Hiding from Bella

Story by Dianne Irving
Photography by Lindsay Edwards

A Harcourt Achieve Imprint

www.Rigby.com
1-800-531-5015

Bella said to Karl,
"I will stay here.
You can go and hide."

"Oh good," said Karl.
"I like hiding."

Bella said, "1, 2, 3, 4, 5."

Karl ran into the house
to hide.

"No running in here!"
said Mom.

Bella shouted, "6, 7, 8, 9, 10 . . . .
here I come."
Bella looked for Karl
in the garden.

"He is not here," she said.
"I will go and look inside."

Bella ran into the house.

"No running in here,"
said Mom.

"Karl is not down here,"
said Bella.
"Here is my doll.
Where is Karl?"

"Dino and Dog
are down here,"
said Bella.

"Where **is** Karl hiding?"

13

"I can see you, Karl."
said Bella.

"You **are** good at hiding."

"I like this game," said Karl.